Colour Land 4

Pupil's Book

erarbeitet von
Doris Höpfl, München
Cornelia Klupp Taylor, Forchheim
Barbara Nirschl, Wackersdorf

Beratung der Bayern-Ausgabe
Barbara Essigkrug, Ismaning
Mira Geiser, Mainberg
Ilka Langlotz-Förtsch, Nürnberg
Susanne Remold, Kammerstein
Silke Richard-Disse, München
Andrea Schöniger, Erlangen
Daniela Schürenberg-Artmann, Diedorf
Sybille Schulze, Triefenstein
Rosi Wagner, Möhrendorf

Ernst Klett Verlag
Stuttgart • Leipzig

So lernen die Kinder mit Colour Land Pupil's Book 4

Jede Unit beginnt mit einer Panorama-Doppelseite.

Hierzu gibt es einen Hörtext auf der Lehrer-CD.

Auf den Wort-Bild-Kärtchen „My words" stehen wichtige Wörter zu den Kapitelthemen.

Wörter des verbindlichen Wortschatzes sind **schwarz**, additional words sind grau gedruckt.

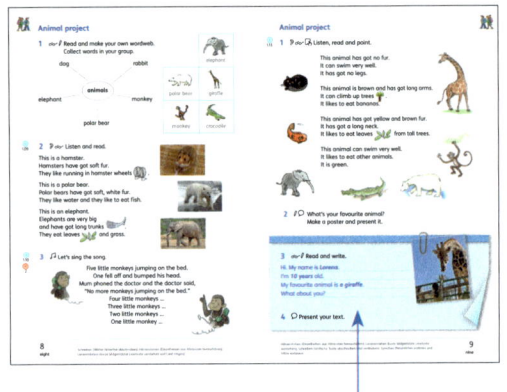

Auf den Übungsseiten gibt es unterschiedliche Aufgaben zum Hören (Hör-/Sehverstehen), Sprechen, Lesen und Schreiben.

Diese Lieder und Reime finden sich auch auf der Schüler-CD im Activity Book.

Nelly zeigt „Nelly's dialogue cards" mit wichtigen Fragen, um Redemittel in Minidialogen zu üben.

Am Ende jeder Unit findet sich ein Text, den die Kinder lesen, abschreiben oder individuell verändern können. Sie können ihren Text der Klasse präsentieren (vorlesen oder frei erzählen).

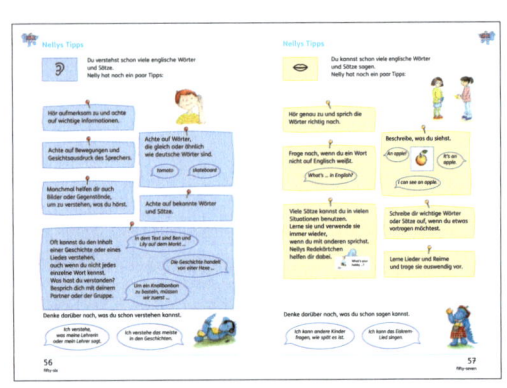

Auf den Methodenseiten gibt Nelly auf Deutsch Tipps zum Erwerb der kommunikativen Kompetenzen sowie zum Erwerb interkultureller Kompetenzen.

Erläuterung der Aufgabensymbole:

✎	Write down.	♫	Let's sing the song.
✐	Draw.	ᴏᴏ	Read.
◯	Talk about .../Present.	Q	Look for information.
◯◯	Talk to your partner.	⚃	Play the game.
ᴐ	Listen.	✂	Fold./Cut.
👆	Point.	**5**	Additional exercise

Im Lernmittel wird in Form von Symbolen auf eine CD verwiesen; diese enthält – bis auf die Hörverstehensübungen – ausschließlich optionale Unterrichtsmaterialien. Die CD unterliegt nicht dem staatlichen Zulassungsverfahren.

Inhaltsverzeichnis

English around the world

1 🎧👆 Listen and point.

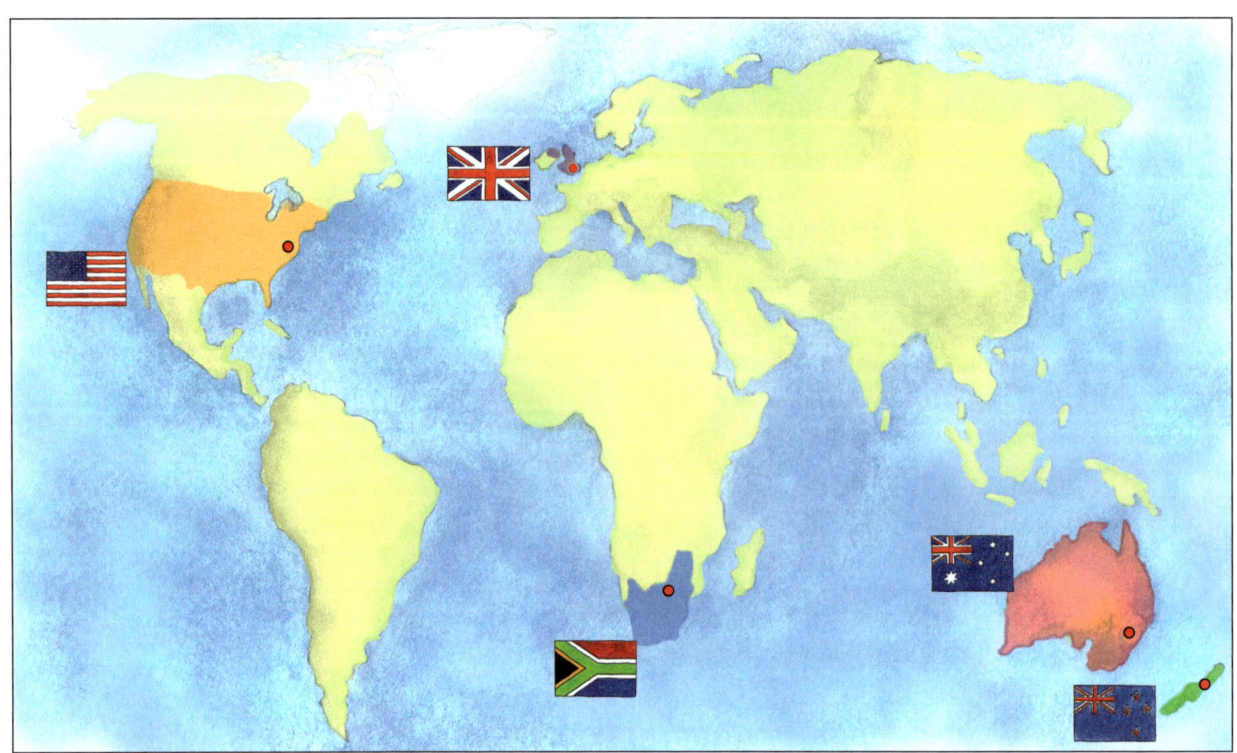

Country:
South Africa

Capital:
Pretoria

Country:
Great Britain

Capital:
London

Country:
Australia

Capital:
Canberra

Country:
New Zealand

Capital:
Wellington

Country:
The United States
of America (USA)

Capital:
Washington D.C.

Hello again!

Interkulturelle Kompetenzen entwickeln (englischsprachige Länder);
Hörverstehen (Einzelheiten aus Hörtexten heraushören)

Let's speak English!

This is my rubber.

And this is my eraser.

1.03

1 🎧👆 Listen and point.

2 💬 Look at the money. What can you see?

3 🗨️💬 Compare £, $ and €. Talk to your group.

Interkulturelle Kompetenzen entwickeln (englischsprachige Länder, Währungen);
Hörverstehen (Einzelheiten aus Hörtexten heraushören); Sprechen (Bilder beschreiben)

5
five

Back to school

1.07

1 💬 Look at the picture. What can you see?

Hör-/Sehverstehen (den wesentlichen Handlungsablauf des Hörtextes mithilfe der Abbildung verstehen);
Sprachmittlung (Hörtext sinngemäß auf Deutsch wiedergeben)

classroom

board

teacher

picture

chair

table

2 What's the story about? Talk to your group. 🇩🇪

Hör-/Sehverstehen (einfache Handlungsanweisungen verstehen, z.B. *Point at Nelly.*);
Sprechen (Fragen beantworten, z.B. *Who is the teacher?*)

7

seven

Animal project

1 ✏️ Read and make your own wordweb.
Collect words in your group.

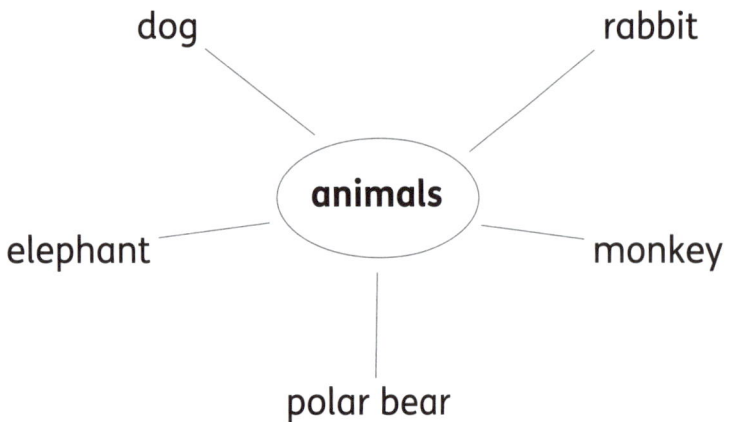

dog · rabbit · **animals** · elephant · monkey · polar bear

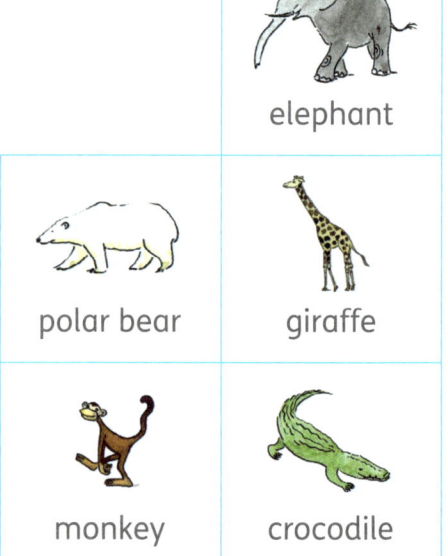

elephant

polar bear · giraffe

monkey · crocodile

1.09

2 🎧 👓 Listen and read.

This is a hamster.
Hamsters have got soft fur.
They like running in hamster wheels  .

This is a polar bear.
Polar bears have got soft, white fur.
They like water and they like to eat fish.

This is an elephant.
Elephants are very big
and have got long trunks  .
They eat leaves  and grass.

1.10
3

3 🎵 Let's sing the song.

Five little monkeys jumping on the bed.
One fell off and bumped his head.
Mum phoned the doctor and the doctor said,
"No more monkeys jumping on the bed."
Four little monkeys ...
Three little monkeys ...
Two little monkeys ...
One little monkey ...

Schreiben (Wörter fehlerfrei abschreiben); Hörverstehen (Einzelheiten aus Hörtexten heraushören);
Leseverstehen (kurze bildgestützte Lesetexte verstehen und Lied singen)

Animal project

1.13

1  Listen, read and point.

This animal has got no fur.
It can swim very well.
It has got no legs.

This animal is brown and has got long arms.
It can climb up trees  .
It likes to eat bananas.

This animal has got yellow and brown fur.
It has got a long neck.
It likes to eat leaves  from tall trees.

This animal can swim very well.
It likes to eat other animals.
It is green.

2 What's your favourite animal?
Make a poster and present it.

3 Read and write.

Hi. My name is *Lorena*.
I'm *10 years* old.
My favourite animal is *a giraffe*.
What about you?

4 Present your text.

Hörverstehen (Einzelheiten aus Hörtexten heraushören); Leseverstehen (kurze bildgestützte Lesetexte
verstehen); Schreiben (einfache Texte abschreiben und verändern); Sprechen (Persönliches erzählen und
Sätze vorlesen)

9
nine

Can you help?

1  Read the dialogues.

I haven't got a **pencil**. Can I have your **pencil**, please?

Yes, here you are.

Thank you.

You're welcome.

I haven't got a **rubber**. Can I have your **rubber**, please?

No, sorry. I haven't got a **rubber**.

It's okay.

2 Talk to your partner.

Can I have ..., please?

1.16

3 Listen and point.

We go to school.

We play and learn.

We help each other.

4

4 Let's sing the song.

Leseverstehen (kurze bildgestützte Lesetexte verstehen); Sprechen (Minidialoge führen);
Hörverstehen (Einzelheiten aus Hörtexten heraushören und Lied singen)

School uniform

1  Look at the pictures. What can you see?

Toby is wearing …

Katy is wearing …

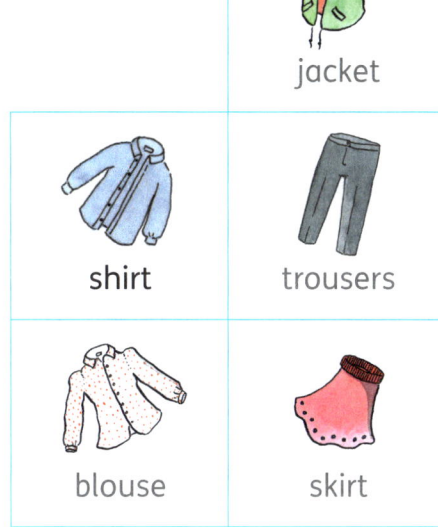

jacket

shirt

trousers

blouse

skirt

2 What do you think about school uniforms?
Talk to your group. 🇩🇪

1.20

3 Listen and point.

4 Read and write.

Good morning.
I'm **George**.
I'm **10** years old.
I'm in **class** 4.
My teacher is **Mr Miller**.
What about you?

5 Present your text.

Sprechen (Bilder beschreiben und Sätze vorlesen); Interkulturelle Kompetenzen entwickeln (Schulleben);
Leseverstehen (kurze Lesetexte verstehen); Schreiben (einfache Texte abschreiben und verändern)

Me and my friends

1.22

1 💬 Look at the picture. What can you see?

Hör-/Sehverstehen (den wesentlichen Handlungsablauf des Hörtextes mithilfe der Abbildung verstehen);
Sprachmittlung (Hörtext sinngemäß auf Deutsch wiedergeben)

boy

girl

friend

children

2 What's the story about? Talk to your group.

Hör-/Sehverstehen (einfache Handlungsanweisungen verstehen, z. B. *Point at Nelly.*);
Sprechen (Fragen beantworten, z. B. *Whose sister is Janet?*)

13
thirteen

Best friends

1.23
8

1  Let's sing the song.

My friend and me, we are a team.
We share our day and our dream.
We play together, jump and run.
We ride our bikes and have much fun.

We are best friends.

1.25

2 Who is it? Listen and point.

3 Read the text.

My friend
It's a boy.
He is wearing a red pullover.
He has got black hair  and brown eyes .
His name is Tom.

4 Describe a boy or a girl in your class.

Hörverstehen (Lied singen und Einzelheiten aus Hörtexten heraushören);
Leseverstehen (kurze Lesetexte verstehen); Schreiben (einfache Texte abschreiben und verändern);
Sprechen (in einfachen Worten beschreiben)

I'm from ...

1.26

1 🎧👆 Who is it? Listen and point.

2 💬 Talk to your partner.

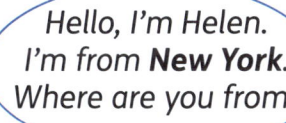

*Hello, I'm Helen. I'm from **New York**. Where are you from?*

*I'm from **London**.*

Where are you from?

3 💬 Make a lapbook and present it to your class.

That's me.

4 👓✏ Read and write.

Hello. My name is *Jason*.

Here is my best friend. His name is *Bill*.

I'm *10* years old.

I'm from *Sydney in Australia*.

Where are you from?

5 💬 Present your text.

Hörverstehen (Einzelheiten aus Hörtexten heraushören); Sprechen (Minidialoge führen, Persönliches erzählen und Sätze vorlesen); Leseverstehen (kurze Lesetexte verstehen); Schreiben (einfache Texte abschreiben und verändern)

15
fifteen

Hobbies and sports

1.28

1 💬 Look at the picture. What can you see?

Hör-/Sehverstehen (den wesentlichen Handlungsablauf des Hörtextes mithilfe der Abbildung verstehen);
Sprachmittlung (Hörtext sinngemäß auf Deutsch wiedergeben)

swimming

playing football

reading books

riding a bike

skateboarding

riding a horse

2 What's the story about? Talk to your group. 🇩🇪

Hör-/Sehverstehen (einfache Handlungsanweisungen verstehen, z. B. *Point at Ben.*);
Sprechen (Fragen beantworten, z. B. *What is Lucy's hobby?*)

17
seventeen

Hobbies

1 Who is it? Listen and say.

Ann

Jim

George

Lorena

2 Read the text.

Ben's hobby is skateboarding  .

Emily's hobby is riding a bike  .

Sally's hobbies are riding a horse and playing football .

Nelly's hobbies are playing tennis and snowboarding .

playing tennis

snowboarding

3 🖊 Make your own wordweb. Collect words in your group.

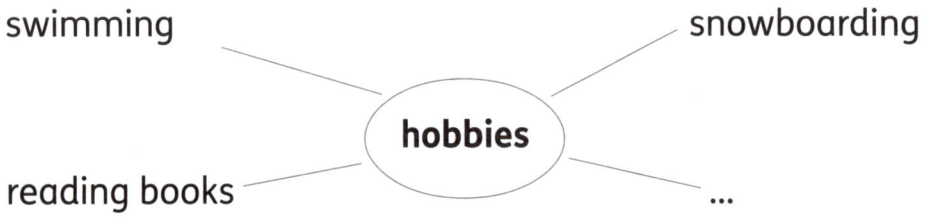

swimming   snowboarding

hobbies

reading books   ...

4 💬 Talk to your partner.

What's your hobby?

What's your hobby?

My hobby is **playing tennis**.

Hörverstehen (Einzelheiten aus Hörtexten heraushören); Leseverstehen (kurze bildgestützte Lesetexte verstehen); Schreiben (Wörter fehlerfrei abschreiben); Sprechen (Minidialoge führen)

My hobby is ...

1 Act out the dialogue.

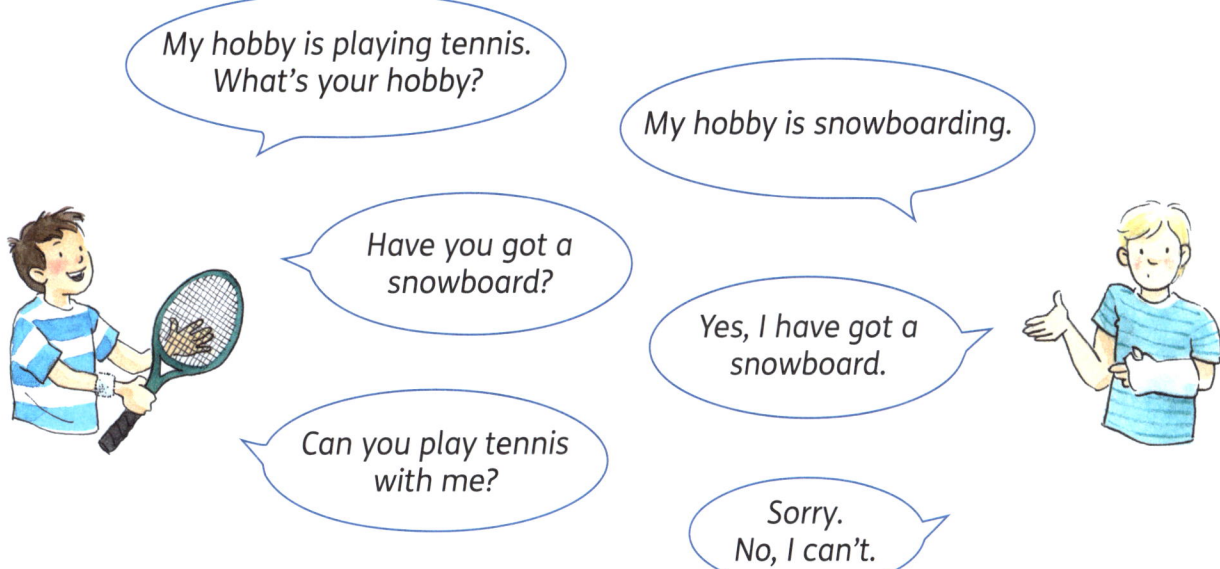

My hobby is playing tennis. What's your hobby?

My hobby is snowboarding.

Have you got a snowboard?

Yes, I have got a snowboard.

Can you play tennis with me?

Sorry. No, I can't.

2  Listen and do the football rap.

1.31
10

Football, football, football is fun!
We can play together, we can kick and run.
We can win or lose,
we don't mind it all.
Eleven in a team,
who like to kick the ball.
Football, football, ...

3 Read and write.

Hi, I'm **Kendra** from **Glasgow**.
My hobbies are **riding a bike** and **playing football**.
I can play **tennis**.
What about you?

4 Present your text.

Sprechen (Minidialoge führen, Lied singen und Sätze vorlesen); Leseverstehen (kurze Lesetexte verstehen);
Schreiben (einfache Texte abschreiben und verändern)

19
nineteen

 # My house

1 💬 Look at the picture. What can you see?

Hör-/Sehverstehen (den wesentlichen Handlungsablauf des Hörtextes mithilfe der Abbildung verstehen);
Sprachmittlung (Hörtext sinngemäß auf Deutsch wiedergeben)

room

house

2 💬 What's the story about? Talk to your group. 🇩🇪

Hör-/Sehverstehen (einfache Handlungsanweisungen verstehen, z.B. *Point at the children's room.*);
Sprechen (Fragen beantworten, z.B. *What's the name of the mouse?*)

21
twenty-one

My house

1.36

1 👂 👓 Listen and read.

Hi, I'm Jane.
This is my mother and my sister.
We live in a big house.

Hello, I'm Safia.
I have got a sister and a brother.
We have got a small house.

1.37

12

2 👂 👓 Listen and read.

My room

I dream in my room and I read in my room.
My wonderful, wonderful room.
I laugh in my room and I cry in my room.
My wonderful, wonderful room.
I close the door and I say to myself,
I'm so happy to be in my room.

3 ✏ Write your own text.

*What's **schlafen** in English?*

*It's **to sleep**.*

Hörverstehen (Einzelheiten aus Hörtexten heraushören); Leseverstehen (kurze bildgestützte Lesetexte verstehen); Schreiben (einfache Texte abschreiben und verändern); Sprechen (unbekannte Wörter nachfragen)

My room

1 ✎ Make your own wordweb. Collect words in your group.

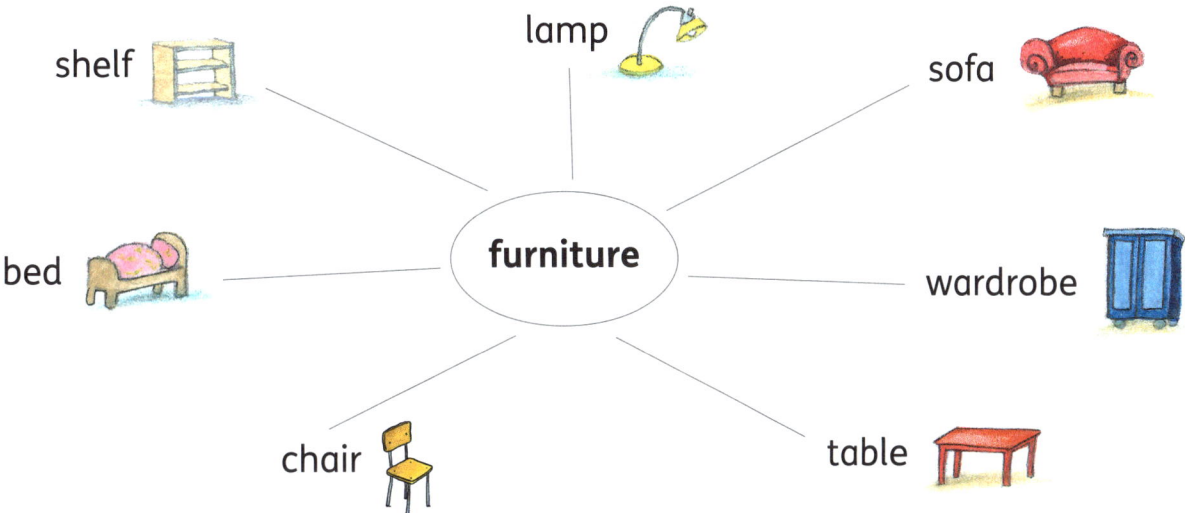

shelf

lamp

sofa

bed

furniture

wardrobe

chair

table

2 ✏️ 💬 Draw your room. Present it.

This is my room.
There is a yellow chair ...

3 👓 ✎ Read and write.

Good morning.
I'm **Katie** from **Chicago**.
I live in a **small house**.
There is a **blue table** in my room.
What about you?

4 💬 Present your text.

Schreiben (Wörter fehlerfrei abschreiben; einfache Texte abschreiben und verändern);
Leseverstehen (kurze Lesetexte verstehen); Sprechen (Persönliches erzählen und Sätze vorlesen)

23
twenty-three

My day

1.40

1 💬 Look at the pictures. What can you see?

Hör-/Sehverstehen (den wesentlichen Handlungsablauf des Hörtextes mithilfe der Abbildungen verstehen); Sprachmittlung (Hörtext sinngemäß auf Deutsch wiedergeben)

play with friends

go to school

morning

afternoon

evening

night

2 **What's the story about? Talk to your group.** 🇩🇪

Hör-/Sehverstehen (einfache Handlungsanweisungen verstehen, z. B. *Point at Ben in school.*);
Sprechen (Fragen beantworten, z. B. *When does Ben go to school?*)

25
twenty-five

What time is it?

1.42

1 Listen and point.

1.43

2 Listen and point.

3 Point and ask your partner.

 What time is it, please?

What time is it, please?

It's **8 o'clock**.

1.44

15

4 Say the tongue twister.

Two witches are watching two watches.
Which witch is watching which watch?

Hörverstehen (Einzelheiten aus Hörtexten heraushören);
Sprechen (Minidialoge führen)

What time is it?

1  Listen and point.

2 Point and ask your partner.

What time is it, please?

*It's **9:45**.*

3 Talk about your day.

*At **1 o'clock** I ...*

*In the **morning** I ...*

4 Read and write.

Hello, I'm **Natasha** from **San Francisco**.
At **7.30** I go to school.
In the **afternoon** I like **skateboarding**.
What about you?

5 Present your text.

Hörverstehen (Einzelheiten aus Hörtexten heraushören); Sprechen (Minidialoge führen, Persönliches erzählen und Sätze vorlesen); Leseverstehen (kurze Lesetexte verstehen); Schreiben (einfache Texte abschreiben und verändern)

The days of the week

1.48
16

1 🎵 Let's sing the song.

The days of the week

The days of the week
are seven in a row.
One, two, three, four, five, six, seven.
The days of the week
how quickly they go:
Monday, Tuesday, Wednesday, Thursday, Friday, Saturday, Sunday!

1.50

2 👂👆 Listen and point.

	Tom's week				weekend	
Monday	Tuesday	Wednesday	Thursday	Friday	Saturday	Sunday

3 ✏️ What about your week? Write and draw.

4 💬 Talk to your partner about your week.

*On **Monday** I ...*

5 💬 What day is it?
How do you feel today?

*Today is **Monday**.
I'm **okay**.*

Hörverstehen (Lied singen und Einzelheiten aus Hörtexten heraushören);
Schreiben (Wörter fehlerfrei abschreiben)

Ben's timetable

1 👓 Look at Ben's timetable.

	MON	TUE	WED	THURS	FRI
9.00	ABC	1+2	🇩🇪	1+2	🏃
10.00	Assembly (all children meet in the school hall)				
10.15	Break				
10.30	1+2	ABC	ABC	1+2	1+2
11.30	🏃	ABC	🏃	ABC	ABC
12.15	Lunchtime				
1.15	✂️	🎵	1+2	🏊	History
2.00	✂️	💻	🔬	🏊	🎵
2.45–3.30	💻	History	🔬	💻	🔬

ABC — English
1+2 — Maths
🇩🇪 — German
🏃 — PE
🎵 — Music
✂️ — Arts and crafts
🔬 — Science
💻 — ICT
History
🏊 — Swimming

2 💬 Compare to your timetable. Talk to your group. 🇩🇪

3 👓🖊 Read and write.

Good morning. I'm **Alfie** from **Belfast**.
I like **Maths** and **Music**.
On **Tuesday** I **play football** in the afternoon.
What about you?

4 💬 Present your text.

Interkulturelle Kompetenzen entwickeln (Schulleben); Leseverstehen (einfache Lesetexte verstehen);
Schreiben (einfache Texte abschreiben und verändern); Sprechen (Sätze vorlesen)

Birthday party

1 Listen and read.

2 Read the letter.

Dear Sally,
my birthday party is on Saturday at 2 o'clock
in the afternoon.
The party is at my house.
Please, come to my party!
Lucy

Interkulturelle Kompetenzen entwickeln (Feste und Bräuche kennen);
Hör-/Sehverstehen (den wesentlichen Handlungsablauf des Hörtextes mithilfe der Abbildung verstehen);
Leseverstehen (kurze bildgestützte Lesetexte verstehen)

Birthday party

1  Talk to your partner.

Can you come to my party?

Can you come to my party?

Yes, thank you.

2  Act out the dialogue.

Hi, James. How are you?

Hello, Ben. I'm fine, thanks. How are you?

I'm fine, thanks. Please, come to my birthday party.

Oh, great. Where is your party?

At my house in High Street number 5.

When is your party?

On Friday at 5 o'clock. Can you come?

Oh, I'm sorry. I can't come.

3 Read and write.

Hello. My name is **Ravi**.
I'm **11** years old. My birthday is in **May**.
For my birthday I'd like a **new football**.
What about you?

4 Present your text.

Sprechen (Minidialoge führen und Sätze vorlesen); Leseverstehen (kurze Lesetexte verstehen);
Schreiben (einfache Texte abschreiben und verändern)

31
thirty-one

Shopping at the market

2.02

1 💬 Look at the picture. What can you see?

Hör-/Sehverstehen (den wesentlichen Handlungsablauf des Hörtextes mithilfe der Abbildung verstehen);
Sprachmittlung (Hörtext sinngemäß auf Deutsch wiedergeben)

RMARKET

Special offer £1

£2

chocolate

sweets

tomato

apple

strawberry

plum

banana

orange

2 💬 What's the story about? Talk to your group.

Hör-/Sehverstehen (einfache Handlungsanweisungen verstehen, z.B. *Point at the apples.*);
Sprechen (Fragen beantworten, z.B. *What is Nelly eating?*)

33
thirty-three

Fruit

1 💬 Look at the picture. What can you see?

2 💬💬 Talk to your partner.

> How much **are the plums**?

> The plums are **£4**.

How much is/are ...?

3 ✏️ Make your own wordweb. Collect words in your group.

apple   plum

fruit

strawberry   ...

grapes   lemon

4 💬 Which fruit do you like?

> I like **apples**. I don't like **plums**.

Sprechen (Bilder beschreiben, Minidialoge führen und Persönliches erzählen);
Schreiben (Wörter fehlerfrei abschreiben)

Fruit

1 👓 Let's make a fruit salad. Read.

Wash and peel the fruit.

Cut the fruit.

Put it in a bowl.

Mix the fruit.

2.06

19

2 🎵 Let's sing the song.

Ice cream, ice cream!
Which one would you like?
Chocolate and banana.
That's what I'd like.

3 👓✏ Read and write.

Hello. I'm **Kiara** and I live in **Manchester**.
I don't like **tomatoes**.
I like **grapes** best.
What's your favourite fruit?

4 💬 Present your text.

Leseverstehen (kurze bildgestützte Lesetexte verstehen); Hörverstehen (Lied singen);
Schreiben (einfache Texte abschreiben und verändern); Sprechen (Sätze vorlesen)

35
thirty-five

Sightseeing in London

2.09

Roll the dice again.

River Thames

Go 3 steps back.

Tower Bridge

Miss a turn.

Tower of London

Big Ben

START

START OF SIGHT-SEEING TOUR

London Eye

1 💬 Look at the picture. What can you see?

Hör-/Sehverstehen (den wesentlichen Handlungsablauf des Hörtextes mithilfe der Abbildung verstehen); Sprachmittlung (Hörtext sinngemäß auf Deutsch wiedergeben); Interkulturelle Kompetenzen entwickeln (englischsprachige Länder)

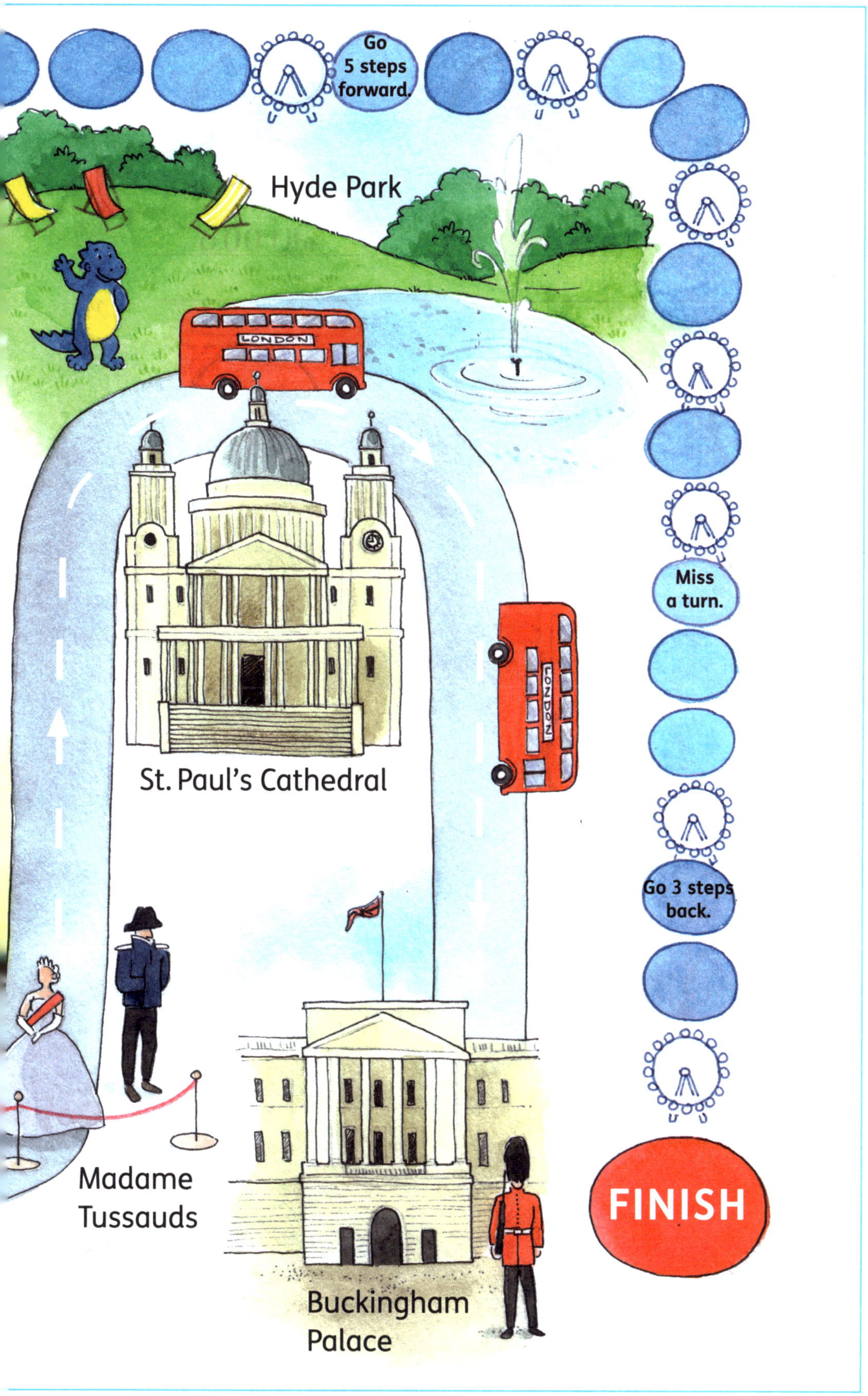

Go
5 steps
forward.

Hyde Park

Miss
a turn.

St. Paul's Cathedral

Go 3 steps
back.

Madame
Tussauds

FINISH

Buckingham
Palace

bus

ticket

2 💬 What's the story about? Talk to your group. 🇩🇪

Hör-/Sehverstehen (einfache Handlungsanweisungen verstehen, z. B. *Point at the Tower Bridge.*);
Sprechen (Fragen beantworten, z. B. *Where is Nelly?*)

37
thirty-seven

In London

1 💬 Look at the pictures. What can you see?

Big Ben

London Eye

Tower Bridge

Tower of London

Buckingham Palace

St. Paul's Cathedral

2 🔍 These are famous buildings in London.
Look for more information. 🇩🇪

3 💬 How do you play the game on page 36/37?
Talk to your group. 🇩🇪

4 🎲 Play the game.

5 🎵 Let's sing the song.

2.10

21

The wheels on the bus go round and round,
round and round, round and round.
The wheels on the bus go round and round,
all day long.

Interkulturelle Kompetenzen entwickeln (englischsprachige Länder); Sprechen (Bilder beschreiben);
Sprachmittlung (einfache Aussagen sinngemäß übertragen: Spielanleitungen, -regeln);
Hörverstehen (Lied singen)

In London

1 How much is a ticket?

A ticket for **St. Paul's Cathedral** is **£ 7**.

2 Act out the dialogue.

How much is/are ...?

Hello, I'd like a ticket for **Madame Tussauds**, please. How much is it?

It's **£ 15.00**.

2.13
22

3 Say the rhyme.

Pussycat

Pussycat, Pussycat, where have you been?
I've been to London to visit the queen.
Pussycat, Pussycat, what did you do there?
I caught a mouse that was under the chair.

4 Read and write.

Hello. My name is **Ethan**.
I live in **London** in a **big** house.
I like **Hyde Park**.
What about you?

5 Present your text.

Sprechen (Minidialoge führen und Sätze vorlesen); Leseverstehen (kurze Lesetexte verstehen); Schreiben (einfache Texte abschreiben und verändern)

39
thirty-nine

Let's celebrate: Halloween

1 🎵 Let's sing the song.

2 🎧 👆 Listen and point.

3 💬 What do you know about sweets at Halloween? Talk to your group. 🇩🇪

Jack-o'-lantern, jack-o'-lantern,
smiling bright, smiling bright,
witches flying in the night.
Halloween, Halloween.

Hörverstehen (Lied singen); Interkulturelle Kompetenzen entwickeln (Feste und Bräuche kennen);
Hör-/Sehverstehen (den wesentlichen Handlungsablauf des Hörtextes mithilfe der Abbildung verstehen)

Let's celebrate: Thanksgiving

1 Listen and read.

2.28

Every year people in the USA celebrate Thanksgiving.
They remember the first harvest festival between the pilgrims and the Indians.
Thanksgiving is on a Thursday in November.
It's a special day for families.
On this day they eat traditional food like turkey, sweet potatoes and pumpkin pie.

2 Listen and read.

2.29

The Thanksgiving story

The pilgrims arrive in America.

The pilgrims are cold and hungry.

The Indians help the pilgrims.

The Indians and the pilgrims celebrate with a big party.

Hör-/Sehverstehen (den wesentlichen Handlungsablauf des Hörtextes mithilfe der Abbildung verstehen); Leseverstehen (kurze bildgestützte Lesetexte verstehen); Interkulturelle Kompetenzen entwickeln (Feste und Bräuche kennen)

41
forty-one

Let's celebrate: Christmas

paper	
toilet roll	
scissors	
glue stick	
wrapping paper	
ribbon	
little presents	

2.31

1 🎧 Listen to the instructions.

2 💬 How to fold the Christmas cracker?
Talk to your group. 🇩🇪

3 ✂ Let's make the Christmas cracker.

① Write a joke or a riddle.

② Make a paper crown.

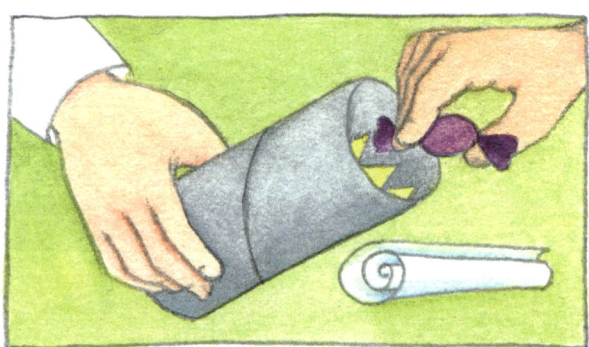

③ Put the crown, the joke and
the present into the roll.

④ Cut out a piece of wrapping
paper.

⑤ Wrap up the toilet roll.

⑥ Decorate your Christmas cracker.

Hör-/Sehverstehen (den wesentlichen Handlungsablauf des Hörtextes mithilfe der Abbildung verstehen);
Leseverstehen (kurze bildgestützte Lesetexte verstehen); Sprachmittlung (Bastelanleitung sinngemäß auf
Deutsch wiedergeben); Interkulturelle Kompetenzen entwickeln (Feste und Bräuche kennen)

Let's celebrate: Summer party

1 ∞ Read the text.

Dear mums and dads,
please come to our summer
party. It's on Friday at 2 o'clock
in the afternoon.
The party is at our school.
Yours, class 4

2.37

28

2 ♫ Let's sing and dance.

Come on friend

1, 2, 3, 4, hello friend,

5, 6, 7, 8, come on friend!

Clap your hands and stamp your feet.

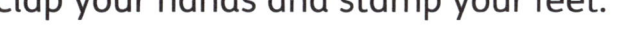

Shake your body and dance to the beat.

Step to the left and step to the right,

alright, alright, alright.

1, 2, 3, 4, hello friend,

5, 6, 7, 8, come on friend!

Snap your finger, jump up high.

Shake your body and do not be shy.

Step to the left and step to the right,

alright, alright, alright.

Leseverstehen (kurze Lesetexte verstehen); Hörverstehen (Lied singen)

Winnie the witch

2.43
2.44

1 🎧 Listen to the story.

① Winnie lives in a black house in the forest.

② She lives there with Wilbur the cat.

③ Winnie sits down on Wilbur, when Wilbur closes his eyes.

④ Winnie trips over Wilbur.

Hör-/Sehverstehen (den wesentlichen Handlungsablauf des Hörtextes mithilfe der Abbildungen verstehen); Sprachmittlung (sinngemäß erklären, worum es in dem Hör- bzw. Lesetext geht)

⑤ Now Wilbur is green.

⑥ But in the garden, Winnie trips again over Wilbur.

⑦ Now Wilbur looks like a rainbow. But Wilbur is not happy.

⑧ Wilbur is black again.

⑨ The house is coloured now. Winnie and Wilbur are happy.

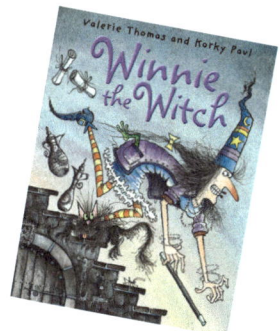

2 💬 What's the story about? Talk to your group.

We're going on a bear hunt

1 🎧 Listen to the story.

We're going on a bear hunt.
We're going to catch a big one.
We're not scared.

Oh, grass.

Oh, a river.

Oh, a storm.

Oh, a forest.

2 💬 What's the story about? Talk to your group.

Hör-/Sehverstehen (den wesentlichen Handlungsablauf des Hörtextes mithilfe der Abbildungen
verstehen); Sprachmittlung (Hörtext sinngemäß auf Deutsch wiedergeben); Sprechen (Texte vortragen:
role play)

Oh, mud.

Oh, a cave.

Aaaah, a bear!

3 💬 Act out the story.

Are you fit for class 5?

1 💬 How do you play the game? Talk to your group.

Sprachmittlung (einfache Aussagen sinngemäß übertragen: Spielanleitungen, -regeln);
Sprechen (Minidialoge führen)

2 🎲 Play the game.

 What's your name?

 How are you?

 What colour is the …?

 How many brothers/sisters have you got?

 How do you feel today?

 Have you got a pet?

 Do you like …?

 What would you like to eat/ to drink?

 When is your birthday?

 How old are you?

 Can I have …, please?

 Where are you from?

 What's your hobby?

 What time is it, please?

 Can you come to my party?

 How much is/are …?

My words – classroom phrases

Listen.

Be quiet, please.

Sit in a circle, please.

Come to the board, please.

Stand up, please.

Sit down, please.

Open your book, please.

Look at the picture.

Point at *the cat*.

Hörverstehen (einfache Handlungsanweisungen verstehen)

My words – classroom phrases

Show me your *book*, please.

Give me the *pencil*, please.

Colour in.

Talk to your partner.

Draw.

Let's sing a song.

Read.

Write down.

Present.

My words – word list

A

a (an)	ein, eine
afternoon	der Nachmittag
and	und
animal	das Tier
apple	der Apfel
April	der April
August	der August
autumn	der Herbst

B

banana	die Banane
to be	sein
bear	der Bär
bed	das Bett
behind	hinter
big	groß
bike	das Fahrrad
birthday	der Geburtstag
black	schwarz
blouse	die Bluse
blue	blau
board	die Tafel
book	das Buch
boy	der Junge
bread	das Brot
breakfast	das Frühstück
brother	der Bruder
brown	braun
budgie	der Wellensittich
bus	der Bus
butter	die Butter
bye	tschüss

C

to can	können
cat	die Katze
chair	der Stuhl
cheese	der Käse
chicken	das Hähnchen
children	die Kinder
chips	die Pommes frites
chocolate	die Schokolade
Christmas	Weihnachten
Christmas cracker	das Knallbonbon
class	die Klasse
classroom	das Klassenzimmer
clothes	die Kleidung
cold	kalt
colour	die Farbe
to come	kommen
crocodile	das Krokodil

D

dear	liebe, lieber
December	der Dezember
to do	tun, machen
dog	der Hund
dress	das Kleid
to drink	trinken

E

to eat	essen
Easter	Ostern
egg	das Ei
elephant	der Elefant
England	England
English	englisch
evening	der Abend

F

family	die Familie
father	der Vater
February	der Februar
fine	gut, schön
fish	der Fisch
football	der Fußball
Friday	der Freitag
friend	der Freund, die Freundin
from	von
fruit	Obst

My words – word list

G

German	deutsch
Germany	Deutschland
giraffe	die Giraffe
girl	das Mädchen
to give	geben
glue stick	der Klebestift
to go	gehen
good	gut
grandfather	der Großvater
grandmother	die Großmutter
grapes	die Weintrauben
great	großartig, super
Great Britain	Großbritannien
green	grün
grey	grau
guinea pig	das Meerschweinchen

H

Halloween	Halloween
ham	der Schinken
hamster	der Hamster
happy	glücklich
to have	haben
he	er
hello	hallo
to help	helfen
her	ihr
here	hier
his	sein
hobby	das Hobby
horse	das Pferd
hot	heiß
house	das Haus
how	wie

I

I	ich
ice cream	die Eiskrem
in	in
in front of	vor

it	es
its	sein

J

jacket	die Jacke
January	der Januar
jeans	die Jeans
July	der Juli
June	der Juni

K

to know	wissen

L

lamp	die Lampe
lemon	die Zitrone
lemonade	die Limonade
to like	mögen
little	klein

M

many	viel, viele
March	der März
May	der Mai
milk	die Milch
Monday	der Montag
monkey	der Affe
morning	der Morgen
mother	die Mutter
mouse	die Maus
much	viel, viele
my	mein

My words – word list

N

name	der Name
next to	neben
night	die Nacht
no	nein
not	nicht
November	der November

O

o'clock (9 o'clock)	Uhrzeit (9 Uhr)
October	der Oktober
okay	gut
old	alt
on	auf
orange	orange
orange	die Orange
orange juice	der Orangensaft

P

party	die Party
pen	der Füller
pencil	der Bleistift
pencil case	das Federmäppchen
pet	das Haustier
picture	das Bild
pig	das Schwein
pink	rosa
to play	spielen
please	bitte
plum	die Pflaume
polar bear	der Eisbär
pullover	der Pullover
purple	lila
to put	legen, stellen, setzen

R

rabbit	das Kaninchen
to read	lesen
red	rot

to ride	reiten
room	der Raum, das Zimmer
rubber	der Radiergummi
ruler	das Lineal

S

sad	traurig
salad	Salat
Saturday	der Samstag
school	die Schule
schoolbag	die Schultasche
September	der September
sharpener	der Spitzer
she	sie
shelf	das Regal
shirt	das Hemd
shoes	die Schuhe
sister	die Schwester
skateboard	das Skateboard
skirt	der Rock
small	klein
snowboard	das Snowboard
socks	die Socken
sofa	das Sofa
sorry	Entschuldigung!
spaghetti	die Spaghetti
sports	die Sportarten
spring	der Frühling
strawberry	die Erdbeere
summer	der Sommer
Sunday	der Sonntag
sweets	die Süßigkeiten
to swim	schwimmen

T

table	der Tisch
to take	nehmen
tea	der Tee
teacher	der Lehrer, die Lehrerin
tennis	das Tennisspiel
thank you, thanks	danke

My words – word list

the	der, die, das
there	dort
they	sie (Plural)
this	dies, diese, dieser
Thursday	der Donnerstag
ticket	die Eintrittskarte
time	die Zeit, die Uhrzeit
tomato	die Tomate
tomato sauce	die Tomatensoße
tomato soup	die Tomatensuppe
trousers	die Hose
T-shirt	das T-Shirt
Tuesday	der Dienstag

U

under	unter

V

very	sehr

W

wardrobe	der Schank
water	das Wasser, das Mineralwasser
we	wir
Wednesday	der Mittwoch
weekend	das Wochenende
welcome	willkommen
what	was
when	wann
where	wo
white	weiß
who	wer
winter	der Winter

Y

year	das Jahr
yellow	gelb
yes	ja
you	du, ihr
your	dein, deine, euer, eure

Nellys Tipps

Du verstehst schon viele englische Wörter und Sätze.
Nelly hat noch ein paar Tipps:

Hör aufmerksam zu und achte auf wichtige Informationen.

Achte auf Wörter, die gleich oder ähnlich wie deutsche Wörter sind.

tomato *skateboard*

Achte auf Bewegungen und Gesichtsausdruck des Sprechers.

Manchmal helfen dir auch Bilder oder Gegenstände, um zu verstehen, was du hörst.

Achte auf bekannte Wörter und Sätze.

Oft kannst du den Inhalt einer Geschichte oder eines Liedes verstehen, auch wenn du nicht jedes einzelne Wort kennst. Was hast du verstanden? Besprich dich mit deinem Partner oder der Gruppe.

In dem Text sind Ben und Lily auf dem Markt ...

Die Geschichte handelt von einer Hexe ...

Um ein Knallbonbon zu basteln, müssen wir zuerst ...

Denke darüber nach, was du schon verstehen kannst.

Ich verstehe, was meine Lehrerin oder mein Lehrer sagt.

Ich verstehe das meiste in den Geschichten.

Nellys Tipps

Du kannst schon viele englische Wörter
und Sätze sagen.
Nelly hat noch ein paar Tipps:

Hör genau zu und sprich die
Wörter richtig nach.

Beschreibe, was du siehst.

Frage nach, wenn du ein Wort
nicht auf Englisch weißt.

What's ... in English?

An apple!

It's an apple.

I can see an apple.

Viele Sätze kannst du in vielen
Situationen benutzen.
Lerne sie und verwende sie
immer wieder,
wenn du mit anderen sprichst.
Nellys Redekärtchen
helfen dir dabei.

What's your hobby ...?

Schreibe dir wichtige Wörter
oder Sätze auf, wenn du etwas
vortragen möchtest.

Lerne Lieder und Reime
und trage sie auswendig vor.

Denke darüber nach, was du schon sagen kannst.

*Ich kann andere Kinder
fragen, wie spät es ist.*

*Ich kann das Eiskrem-
Lied singen.*

Nellys Tipps

 Du kannst bereits einige englische Wörter und Sätze lesen.
Nelly hat noch ein paar Tipps:

Achte auf bekannte Wörter.

Achte auf Wörter, die gleich oder ähnlich geschrieben werden, wie deutsche Wörter.

April – April,
hobby – Hobby

Oft kannst du den Inhalt eines Textes verstehen, auch wenn du nicht jedes einzelne Wort kennst.
Was hast du verstanden? Besprich dich mit deinem Partner oder der Gruppe.

Manchmal helfen dir auch Bilder, einen Text zu verstehen.

Auf einem Arbeitsblatt kannst du auch wichtige Wörter im Text markieren.

Schlag unbekannte Wörter nach.

hamster	monkey	grapes

Du kannst auch ein Bildwörterbuch benutzen. Hier sind die Wörter nach Themen geordnet.

Lies Wörter und Sätze vor. Oft werden gleiche Buchstaben unterschiedlich ausgesprochen.

mother, cold, ...

Denke darüber nach, was du schon lesen kannst.

> Ich kann die Obstsorten lesen.

> Ich kann kurze Texte vorlesen.

Nellys Tipps

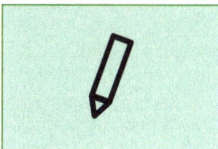

Du kannst schon einige englische Wörter und Sätze schreiben.
Nelly hat noch ein paar Tipps:

Lies das Wort und präge es dir ein.
Schreibe das Wort auswendig auf und vergleiche anschließend.

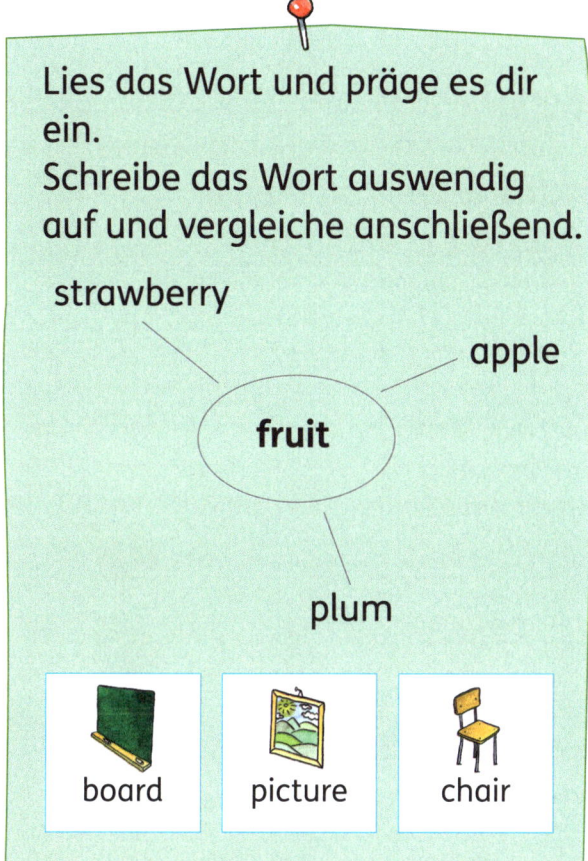

strawberry

apple

fruit

plum

board   picture   chair

Denke daran, dass Nomen im Plural meistens ein s haben.

1 chair – 2 chairs

Schreibe Wörter auf und markiere schwierige Stellen.

blue, father, ...

Denke daran, dass viele Wörter anders geschrieben werden, als du sie sprichst.

mother, father, ...

Beachte, dass die meisten Nomen kleingeschrieben werden.

boy, girl, ...

Du kannst auch ein Bildwörterbuch benutzen. Hier sind die Wörter nach Themen geordnet.

Denke darüber nach, was du schon schreiben kannst.

Ich kann Tiere abschreiben.

Ich kann einen Steckbrief abschreiben und ändern.

Nellys Tipps

Du weißt schon viel über Großbritannien, die Vereinigten Staaten von Amerika und die englische Sprache.
Nelly hat noch ein paar Tipps:

Verwende typische englische Sätze zur Begrüßung und zur Verabschiedung.

Hello!   *Bye-bye!*

Lerne englische Lieder und Reime kennen.

The wheels on the bus go round and round ...

Vergleiche britische und amerikanische Feste mit deinen Festen.

Der Weihnachtsmann bringt Geschenke mit einem Rentier-Schlitten.

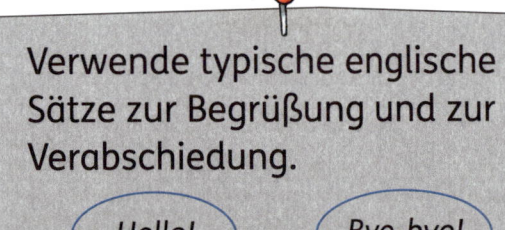

Informiere dich in Sachbüchern oder im Internet über Großbritannien und die USA: Landschaften, Städte, Gerichte, berühmte Personen, Sportarten, ...

Thanksgiving?
Ich suche Informationen im Internet mithilfe einer Kinder-Suchmaschine.

Tausche dich mit einem Partner aus.

Der Amerikaner Neil Armstrong war der erste Mensch auf dem Mond.

Ich weiß, dass die Tower Bridge eine berühmte Brücke in London ist.

Gestaltet in der Gruppe ein Plakat.
Präsentiert euer Plakat der Klasse.

Very British!
– Königsfamilie
– Scotland, Wales, ...
– ...